It's easy to forget, safe on dry land, that
nearly three-quarters of Earth's surface is covered
with water — most of which is more than a half mile deep.

The oceans are full of creatures, from microscopic plankton to
gigantic blue whales — creatures that are beautiful, hideous,
gentle, or lethal — but never less than fascinating.

**Hold the special 3-D
glasses in front of your eyes.
Prepare to dive beneath
the waves and meet . . .**

Seabirds

No bird lives its life entirely at sea. They must all return to land to breed. But there are many birds, such as the albatross, that drink seawater, sleep while flying, and spend very little time on land.

Animals of the Frozen Poles

The two poles are very different places. The North Pole, or Arctic, is a vast, permanent ice cap floating on the Arctic Ocean. The South Pole, or Antarctica, is a continent in its own right — an enormous landmass, covered with an ice sheet twice the size of the United States. Although both poles are hostile, freezing places to live, many creatures have evolved against the odds to thrive there.

Sea Reptiles

Despite breathing air and, in most cases, needing to return to land to breed, many reptiles are well adjusted to life at sea. Reptiles are often said to be cold-blooded. This does not mean their blood is always cold. It means they are only as warm or as cold as their surroundings. For this reason, sea reptiles live only in relatively warm seas.

Dolphins and Whales

Dolphins and whales have always fascinated people — dolphins, for their intelligence and friendliness to humans, and whales, for their size and majesty. Both are mammals like us, which means that they are warm-blooded and give birth to live young, which they feed with milk.

Sharks: Killers of the Deep

When most people think "shark," they think of the terrifying great white, but there are many different species. All sharks do have things in common, too. They all have skeletons made of cartilage, a hard substance that is lighter than bone. They all have skin that is covered in tiny bumps, making them rough to touch. And they are all predators, eating live prey in one form or another. Many species are in danger of becoming extinct — more than 100 million are killed by fishermen each year!

Coral Reefs

Coral polyps are tiny creatures with sacklike bodies. They have hard skeletons on the outside of their bodies, called exoskeletons. Living polyps attach their exoskeletons to those of dead polyps and then die themselves. This is repeated, and over thousands of years these mounds of exoskeletons form what we call coral reefs.

Creatures of the Deep

The ocean's deepest point occurs in the Pacific Ocean, where the seabed can be nearly seven miles from the surface. At such depths, sunlight cannot penetrate and the immense water pressure could crush steel. Yet even in these hostile conditions, there is life.

Penguin

- The majority of penguins live in Antarctica. They are not found at the North Pole.
- Emperor penguins are the largest of all penguins.
- Emperor penguins can weigh up to 88 pounds, which is about the same as a 14-year-old child.
- To cope with the extreme cold, emperor penguins huddle together in huge groups, frequently swapping places so that no single penguin spends too long at the exposed edge.

Albatross

- Some albatrosses have wingspans of nearly 11.5 feet — the largest of any bird.
- Albatrosses flap their enormous wings very little. Instead, they glide on air currents. In calm conditions, they must rest on the surface of the sea.
- Because predators rarely catch them, they are among the few birds to die of old age.
- Superstitious sailors used to believe that killing an albatross would bring bad luck.

Tiger Shark

- The tiger shark is a large and aggressive shark — some reach 20 feet in length.
- A fierce hunter and tireless scavenger, the tiger shark will eat almost anything — including people.
- Strange things such as dogs, deer antlers, and bottles have been found in their stomachs.
- The tiger shark is found in warm oceans, from the shoreline to the open sea.

Humpback Whale

- The humpback whale is recognizable by its bumpy head and long flippers.
- Each humpback has a unique set of markings on the underside of its tail.
- They are natural show-offs and seem happy to entertain whale watchers by leaping out of the water.
- Humpbacks can reach 50 feet in length and weigh up to 30 tons — that's more than a tank!

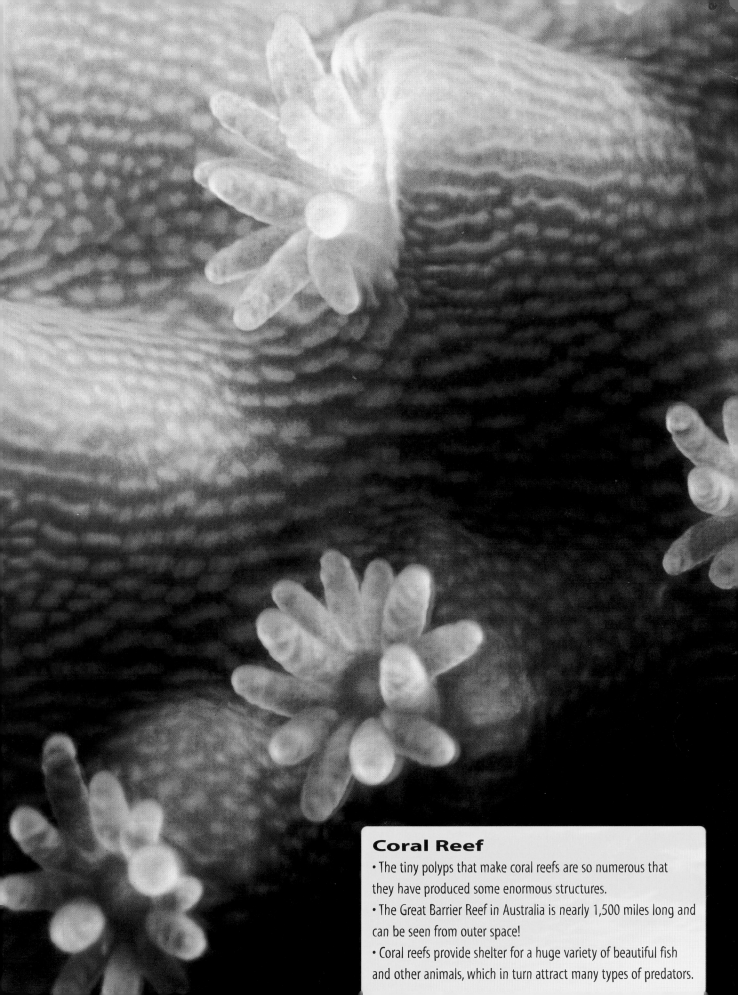

Coral Reef
• The tiny polyps that make coral reefs are so numerous that they have produced some enormous structures.
• The Great Barrier Reef in Australia is nearly 1,500 miles long and can be seen from outer space!
• Coral reefs provide shelter for a huge variety of beautiful fish and other animals, which in turn attract many types of predators.

Anglerfish

- Anglerfish have stomachs that expand to enable them to swallow prey larger than themselves.
- Anglerfish can live at depths of up to 2.5 miles.
- This is a male anglerfish. Females have a longer spike at the front of their heads. This attracts fish that mistake it for prey. These fish soon become prey themselves.

Turtle

- Turtles feed on plants and fish and have even been known to pluck resting seabirds from the waves.
- The leatherback is the largest of all turtles. It can reach nearly 10 feet in length and weigh more than a half ton.
- Turtles can live to be 100 years old.

Puffin

- The puffin belongs to a family of birds called auks.
- Puffins eat small fish such as sand eels, capelin, and small cod.
- Puffins are found in large numbers on North Atlantic and Arctic coastlines.

Dolphin

- Dolphins are highly intelligent, social animals that live in groups called pods.
- They communicate with one another using a complex language of clicks and whistles.
- Dolphins locate their prey in the same way as bats by making clicking noises or "sonic pulses." The length of time the noises take to return to the dolphin tells it how far away its prey is.

Squid

- The squid is an invertebrate, which means that it has no backbone.
- Squid are intelligent creatures with well-developed brains and three hearts.
- When attacked, they spray clouds of ink into the water to mask their escape.
- Like chameleons, the squid can change color to blend in with its surroundings.

Polar Bear

- Polar bears live on the edges of the North Pole and can be found as far south as Canada.

- They can reach a weight of a half ton and a height of 6.5 feet. They are the Arctic's most ferocious hunters.

- They are excellent swimmers and stay close to the shore, where they hunt their favorite prey — seals.

- Each polar bear hair is hollow. This hollow hair traps bubbles of warm air above the skin, which help keep out the cold.

Lionfish

- This brightly colored fish is usually found in coral reefs, especially in the shallow waters of the Indian and Pacific oceans.

- Each species has a particular pattern of zebralike stripes.

- Lionfish have poisonous fin spines that can produce painful puncture wounds.

- Although these stings can cause nausea and breathing difficulties, they are rarely fatal to humans.

Saltwater Crocodile

• The saltwater or estuarine crocodile can reach more than 23 feet in length and can weigh up to one ton.

• Estuarine crocodiles can live in coastal areas because they have evolved to survive in salty water.

• They are able to travel long distances at sea.

• Their diet consists mainly of birds, fish, and mammals, but they have been known to kill and eat large sharks.

Mysidacea

- Mysids, as they are commonly called, are members of the crustacean family, like crabs, lobsters, and shrimp.
- Most are found at depths below a half mile.
- The mysid's red body is perfectly camouflaged in the deep, dark sea where no red light penetrates and red colors look black.
- They have an armored shell to protect them from predators.

Great White Shark

• Great whites are really gray or brown with white undersides.

• They can reach up to 23 feet in length and two tons in weight — that's as much as two cars!

• Great whites have a very diverse diet, which includes fish, other sharks, porpoises, and, occasionally, humans!

• They kill more people than any other type of shark.

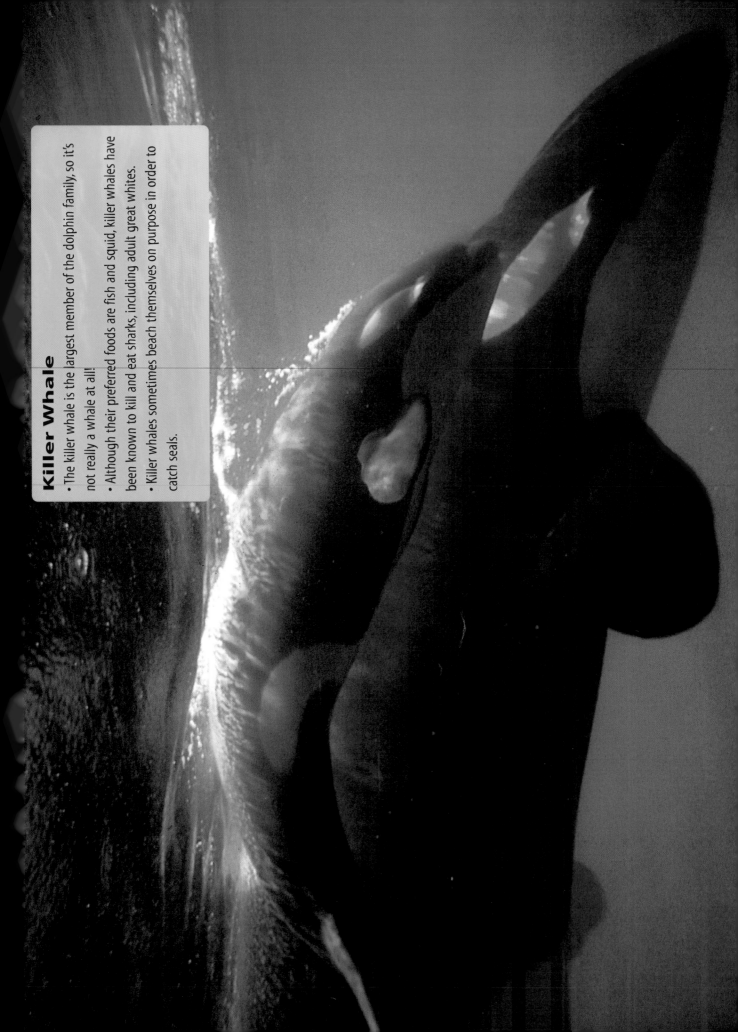

Killer Whale

- The killer whale is the largest member of the dolphin family, so it's not really a whale at all!
- Although their preferred foods are fish and squid, killer whales have been known to kill and eat sharks, including adult great whites.
- Killer whales sometimes beach themselves on purpose in order to catch seals.

Sea Snake

• Sea snakes look the same as land snakes, except for a flattened tail that acts as a rudder.
• They have special lungs to allow them to remain underwater for long periods of time.
• Sea snakes feed on fish, fish eggs, and eels.
• They have the most lethal poison of all snakes.

Crown-of-thorns Starfish

• These beautiful starfish can reach nearly three feet in diameter.

• Their spines give painful wounds to any creature foolish enough to touch them.

• The crown-of-thorns starfish can shed a limb if a predator seizes it and then regrow it later.

• They eat algae and large amounts of coral.

Hammerhead Shark

• The hammerhead shark gets its name from the shape of its head.

• Its unusually shaped head may give it a wider field of vision and help it to steer.

• Hammerhead sharks are swift, powerful predators. They feed on fish, squid, stingrays, and other sharks.

Walrus

- These tusked, blubbery creatures live only in the Arctic.
- They like to live in shallow water near ice floes or land.
- A walrus's diet includes clams, snails, crabs, shrimp, and worms.
- The number of rings on a walrus's teeth shows its age, like a tree. They have been known to live up to 35 years.

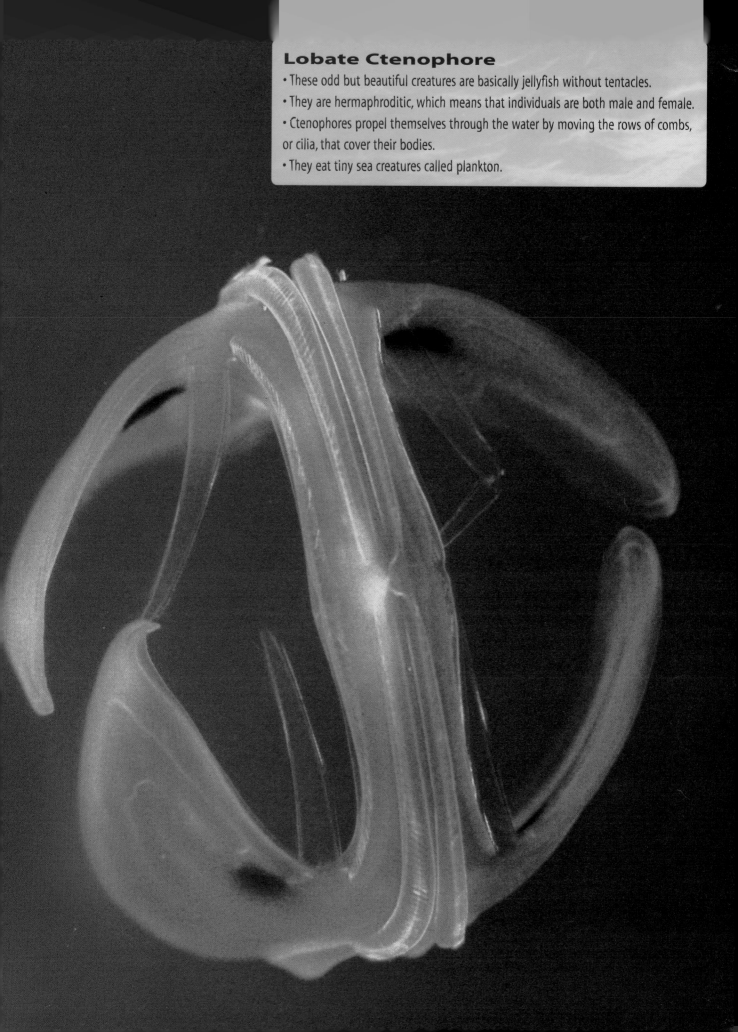

Lobate Ctenophore

- These odd but beautiful creatures are basically jellyfish without tentacles.
- They are hermaphroditic, which means that individuals are both male and female.
- Ctenophores propel themselves through the water by moving the rows of combs, or cilia, that cover their bodies.
- They eat tiny sea creatures called plankton.

Sally Lightfoot Crab

• The Sally Lightfoot crab was named by sailors in honor of a nineteenth-century dancer because it moves with such speed and grace.

• Young Sally Lightfoot crabs are black, which makes them hard for predators to spot among the wet rocks where they live.

• They feed mainly on algae.

• They live on rocky shores around the Atlantic and Pacific oceans.

PRINCESS TRULY in

I Am Truly

For my girls, I love you big!

— K.G.

For Junie and Jalen.

You are Truly fierce and fabulous!

— A.R.

PRINCESS TRULY
in
I Am Truly

by
Kelly Greenawalt

illustrated by
Amariah Rauscher

Scholastic Inc.

I am Truly.

I like frogs
and the color blue.
I can climb trees
and be a rock star, too.

I can run fast
and build tall towers.

I am a superhero
with magical powers.

I am smart,

I am studious,

I am a high achiever.

I am strong,
I am skillful,
I am a born leader.

I can sail the seas
on a little boat.
I can eat every bite
of a root beer float.

I can tie
my own shoes.
I can find treasure
with clues.

I am clever,
I am curious,
I am an engineer.

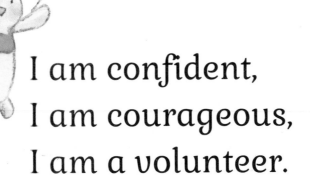

I am confident,
I am courageous,
I am a volunteer.

I can fly to the moon

and dance on the stars.

I can tame wild lions
and race fast cars.

I can swim like a fish.
I can shoot and swish.

I am funny,
I am flexible,
I am an entertainer.

I am focused,
I am fierce,
I am a dinosaur trainer.

I can grow
purple grapes.
I can create
amazing shapes.

I can feed
hungry bunnies
crunchy carrots.

I can learn
Japanese
and teach it
to parrots.

I am Truly, watch me soar.
I am small but mighty,
hear me R R R R R R ROO

oARR!

I can do anything
I set my mind to do.

Do you know that you
can do all these things, too?

You are Truly Fabulous!

Dear Readers:

We created Princess Truly for our daughters. We wanted them to see a strong, smart, problem-solving, confident young girl with beautiful curls who could do anything she set her mind to! We hope these books inspire readers everywhere to reach for the stars, dream big, and stay TRUE to who they are.

Kelly

Amariah

Kelly and her daughters,
Calista and Kaia

Amariah with her daughters,
Jalen and Junie